World Almanac® Library of

THE HOLOCAUST

Aftermath and Remembrance

David Downing

WORLD ALMANAC® LIBRARY

Please visit our web site at: www.worldalmanaclibrary.com
For a free color catalog describing World Almanac® Library's list of
high-quality books and multimedia programs, call 1-800-848-2928 (USA)
or 1-800-387-3178 (Canada). World Almanac® Library's fax: (414) 332-3567.

Library of Congress Cataloging-in-Publication Data

Downing, David, 1946-
    Aftermath and remembrance / by David Downing.
        p. cm. — (World Almanac Library of the Holocaust)
    Includes bibliographical references and index.
    ISBN 0-8368-5948-0 (lib. bdg.)
    ISBN 0-8368-5955-3 (softcover)
    1. Holocaust, Jewish (1939-1945)—Influence—Juvenile literature. 2. Holocaust,
Jewish (1939-1945)—Moral and ethical aspects—Juvenile literature. 3. Holocaust
survivors—Juvenile literature. I. Title. II. Series.
    D804.34.D678   2005
    940.53'1814—dc22   2005040781

First published in 2006 by
World Almanac® Library
A Member of the WRC Media Family of Companies
330 West Olive Street, Suite 100
Milwaukee, WI 53212 USA

Produced by Discovery Books
Editors: Geoff Barker, Sabrina Crewe, and Jacqueline Gorman
Designer and page production: Sabine Beaupré
Photo researchers: Geoff Barker and Rachel Tisdale
Map: Stefan Chabluk
Consultant: Ronald M. Smelser, Professor of Modern German History, University of Utah
World Almanac® Library editorial direction: Mark J. Sachner
World Almanac® Library editor: Alan Wachtel
World Almanac® Library art direction: Tammy West
World Almanac® Library production: Jessica Morris

Photo credits: cover: Patrick Kovarik/AFP/Getty Images; title page: David Press; p. 4: USHMM, courtesy
of National Archives; p. 7: David E. Scherman/Time Life Pictures/Getty Images; p. 8: USHMM, courtesy
of Erica & Joseph Grossman; p. 13: Keystone/Getty Images; p. 14: Topfoto.co.uk; p. 17: USHMM, courtesy
of Vitka Kempner Kovner; p. 19: USHMM, courtesy of Gerald (Gerd) Schwab; p. 20: Keystone/Getty
Images; p. 21: Thomas D. Mcavoy/Time Life Pictures/Getty Images; p. 24: USHMM, courtesy of Israel
Government Press Office; p. 26: Topfoto.co.uk; p. 27: Topfoto.co.uk; p. 29: Jeff Greenberg/The Image
Works/Topfoto.co.uk; p. 30: Eric Feferberg/AFP/Getty Images; p. 33: Topfoto.co.uk; p. 35: USHMM,
courtesy of Archiwum Panstwowego Museum na Majdanek; p. 37: Scott Peterson/Getty Images; p. 38:
Alex Wong/Getty Images; p. 41: Eitan Abramovich/AFP/Getty Images; p. 42: Corbis; p. 43: Corbis.

Printed in Canada

1 2 3 4 5 6 7 8 9 09 08 07 06 05

Cover: President Chirac of France (front row, right) and Simone Veil, former Auschwitz prisoner and
French health minister (front row, second right), attend a ceremony marking the sixtieth anniversary
of the liberation of the Auschwitz death camp in January 2005.

Title page: A synagogue museum in Budapest, Hungary, displays reminders of the Holocaust. As
part of their campaign to humiliate their victims, Nazis forced Jewish prisoners in camps to denigrate
sacred objects by making dresses from prayer shawls and drumheads out of Torah scrolls.

Contents

The Holocaust

The Murder of Millions

The word *holocaust* has a long history. In early times, it meant a burnt offering to the gods, and in the **Middle Ages**, a huge sacrifice or destruction. It still has this second meaning today, particularly when used to describe large-scale destruction by fire or nuclear weapons. But since the 1970s, the word has gained a new and specific meaning. Today, when people refer to the Holocaust—with a capital "H"—they mean the murder of approximately six million Jews by Nazi Germany and its **allies** during World War II.

This crime had deep historical roots. In predominantly Christian Europe, the Jews had always been considered a race apart and had often endured persecution for that reason. When governments or peoples wanted someone to blame for misfortune, they often picked on an innocent, but helpless, Jewish minority.

In the early twentieth century, many Germans wanted some-one to blame for their defeat in World War I and the terrible

Dachau concentration camp survivors cheer their American liberators on April 29, 1945.

economic hardship that followed. They, too, picked on the Jews in their midst—with ultimately horrific results. The Holocaust was ordered and organized by political leaders, carried out by thousands of their willing supporters, and allowed to happen by millions of ordinary people.

The scale of the crime is still hard to take in. To use a modern comparison, about three thousand people were killed in the **terrorist** attacks in the United States on September 11, 2001. Between June 1941 and March 1945, an average of four thousand European Jews were murdered every day.

These people were killed in a variety of ways. Some were left to starve, some to freeze. Many were worked to death in **labor camps**. More than one million were shot and buried in mass graves. Several million were gassed to death in specially built **extermination camps** such as Auschwitz and Treblinka.

The Persecution of the Jews

Jews were not the only victims of the Nazis. In fact, it is probable that the Nazis and their allies murdered at least five million other **civilians** before and during World War II. Their victims were killed for a variety of reasons: **communists** for their political opinions, **homosexuals** for their sexual orientation, people with mental disabilities for their supposed uselessness to society, **Gypsies** and Slavs for their supposed racial inferiority, and Russians, Poles, and other eastern Europeans because they happened to be in the Nazis' way.

The central crime in the Holocaust—the murder of millions of Jews—was a long time in the making. Most of the actual killing took place between 1941 and 1945, but the Jews of Germany were subject to intense persecution from the moment Adolf Hitler and his Nazi Party took power in 1933. That persecution was itself merely the latest in a series of persecutions stretching back over almost two thousand years, in which every nation of Europe had at some time played a part.

This book looks at the aftermath of the Holocaust, at what happened to survivors and to those responsible. It examines the Holocaust's legacy and the ways its victims are remembered.

CHAPTER ONE

The Survivors

Europe After the War

By the spring of 1945, Nazi Germany was facing certain defeat. On April 30, Adolf Hitler committed suicide in Berlin, and in the week that followed, German commanders on the various fronts surrendered to the Allies.

After six years of war, Europe was in a terrible mess. A high proportion of industrial plants and transportation links had been either badly damaged or completely destroyed. Millions of homes had been reduced to rubble or ashes. As many as forty million people had been killed, and the movements of armies and the demands of the German war economy had uprooted millions more. The first months of peace found the continent

A Cruel Homecoming

"I arrived in Krakow around noon. . . . I saw a man who was still wearing the stripes from the concentration camp. As I tried to approach him, two Polish people started to question him. 'Hey Jew, where are you going? Why aren't you going to Palestine? We don't want you here!' I was dumbfounded. I saw tears come down the man's face and nobody came to his defense. I was scared too, and angry. How dare they? Yes, I am a Jew, but I am also a Pole. How dare they? I felt that the multitude of people were looking at me. I met their glare of hate with my own hate. I felt like shouting at them: 'You didn't help us; you turned us in; you are worse than the Germans.'"

Victor Breitburg, a survivor of the Lodz Ghetto,
describing his return home to Krakow after World War II

Polish women gather to sing hymns at a United Nations' refugee camp in Allied-occupied Germany.

full of **refugees**, many of them hungry, sick, and deeply upset by their wartime experiences.

Lost and Alone

Among these millions were about 200,000 Jewish survivors of the Holocaust. As the Soviet, British, and U.S. armies advanced through Nazi Germany, many Jews were liberated from numerous concentration camps and labor camps. Others were found wandering the countryside, having been abandoned by their Nazi guards. Thousands more nervously emerged from hiding, some after spending years hidden in cramped spaces, far from the light of day.

They had survived, but they had little else to feel good about. Most knew, or soon discovered, that the other members of their families had been killed. Many had also lost their homes and their means of making a living. Almost all were in poor physical health—in the camps, in fact, prisoners kept

"The Boys"

When the Theresienstadt concentration camp in Czechoslovakia was liberated in 1945, several thousand teenage orphans, most of whom were from Poland, were among those set free. The British government agreed to take in one thousand of them, and during the second half of 1945, "the Boys" (as they were called, despite the presence of several girls among them)

Four of "the Boys" pose for the camera. They and 728 other orphans (80 of them girls) were brought from Prague to Britain between August 1945 and June 1946.

were flown in bombers to the Lake District in Britain. The first group arrived in August that year.

A Jewish journalist, Joseph Finklestone, was one of the people who witnessed their arrival in Britain at the small country airport. He had been told that "some young people" were coming, but not who they were. "Only when I saw the boys and girls," he wrote later, "in their ill-fitting clothes, tense as they entered a new world, did I suddenly realize with a pang that they had experienced the greatest human-made hell in history. They had seen their parents, sisters and brothers shot, starved and gassed by the Nazis."

dying long after the day of liberation—and most, not surprisingly, were mentally **traumatized** by all that had happened to them. Different individuals felt different combinations of loss, insecurity, and anger. Many people felt guilty for surviving when so many others had not.

With No Direction Home

The first instinct of survivors was to go home. This was possible for some, although the home they went back to could never be the same. Otto Frank, the father of Anne Frank (the Jewish girl whose famous diary survived her own death in Bergen-Belsen concentration camp), survived his time in Auschwitz and returned to Amsterdam in the Netherlands to find that his employees had kept his business running for him. The rest of his family, however, had all been killed.

For most Jews, it was hard—impossible, in many cases—to reclaim their homes and businesses. Poland proved particularly unwelcoming to them. More than one thousand Jews who returned to their homes in Poland after the war were murdered in the first year of peace by gangs of **anti-Semitic** thugs. When forty-two camp survivors were murdered by a mob in the town of Kielce on July 4, 1946, it became clear that there was little hope of recreating a safe Jewish community in Poland. They would have to find a new life elsewhere.

Displaced Persons

Most Jewish survivors of the Holocaust spent many months and often years in the numerous **Displaced Persons (DP) camps** that had been set up across Europe. Only a few DPs went back to their original towns and villages in Poland, western Ukraine, Byelorussia, and Lithuania, which were still full of anti-Semites and some of which were under Soviet control. Most wanted to leave Europe behind and make a new start elsewhere in the world. The most favored destinations—the United States and Palestine—were taking in only a limited number of **immigrants** each year, but most survivors were prepared to wait in the DP camps until they could have the life they really wanted.

CHAPTER TWO

Founding Israel in Palestine

A New Start

The idea of **Zionism**—the movement to establish a new, independent homeland for the Jewish people in Palestine—was more than half a century old when World War II ended. Not surprisingly, the terrible Jewish losses of the Holocaust gave added strength and urgency to this idea. The Zionists argued that only in such a homeland could Jews find the freedom, peace, and security that had so long been denied to them in many parts of Europe. Representatives of the Jews already in Palestine toured the DP camps, urging their fellow Jews to join them in the struggle to found a Jewish state. Many non-Jews supported Jewish **emigration** to Palestine. Some did this from a blatant anti-Semitic desire to get rid of the Jews, others from a guilty belief that Europe owed the Jews something after the horrors of the Holocaust.

One Home

"You must follow my route. It is the only one for the Jewish people. . . ."

Holocaust survivor Abba Naor, writing to his father soon after his liberation from the Dachau concentration camp and shortly before he left for Palestine. The quotation is positioned at the entrance to the Yad Vashem Museum Holocaust Memorial complex in Jerusalem, Israel.

Palestine before 1947

Palestine is often referred to as "the Holy Land" because of the places there, notably the city of Jerusalem, that

To Be Free of Fear

"We want only that which is given naturally to all people of the world, to be masters of our own fate—*only* of our own fate, not of the destiny of others; to live as of right and not on sufferance, to have the chance to bring surviving Jewish children, of whom not so many are left in the world now, to this country [Palestine] so that they may grow up like youngsters who were born here, free of fear, with heads high."

Zionist leader Golda Meir, speaking in 1946.
She became prime minister of Israel in 1969.

are important and sacred sites in the Jewish, Muslim, and Christian religions. The Palestine region had been a Jewish homeland almost two thousand years before the Zionist movement began, but other peoples and states had existed there both before, during, and since that period. In the late nineteenth century, before Zionist **immigration** to Palestine gathered speed, the area—then a province of Ottoman Turkey—was almost entirely populated by Arabs. During World War I, the British, with significant help from their Arab allies, defeated the Ottoman Turks and removed them from the area.

In 1915, in return for the Arabs' help, the British had promised to "recognize and support independence" for Arabs in the Middle East. Britain failed to honor that promise when it made an agreement—the Sykes-Picot Agreement of 1916—with France the following year to divide the Arab lands between the two European nations. (The area of Palestine, with its holy sites, would be under joint rule.)

Then, in the Balfour Declaration of 1917, Britain's foreign minister Arthur Balfour apparently contradicted both these agreements. He promised to "view with favor" the establishment of a Jewish "national home" in Palestine.

In 1919, these various agreements and promises were put to one side. Britain received a **mandate** from a new international body, the League of Nations, to administer the area of Palestine, Transjordan, and Iraq from 1920. The British were supposed to prepare the territories for independence. During the next seventeen years, Iraq and Transjordan did become independent. In Palestine, meanwhile, both Jewish immigration and the resulting Arab resentment grew. The British, trusted by neither side, struggled but failed to keep the peace.

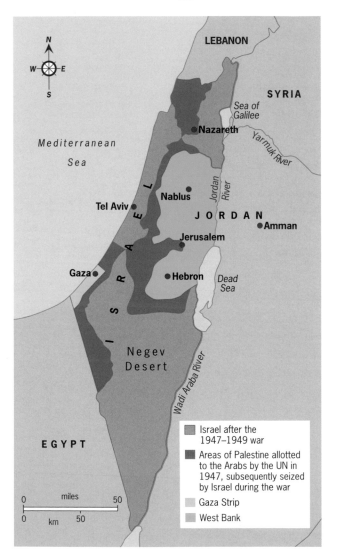

Israel after the 1947–1949 war

Areas of Palestine allotted to the Arabs by the UN in 1947, subsequently seized by Israel during the war

Gaza Strip

West Bank

After World War II

By the end of World War II, the population of Palestine was about 70 percent Arab, 30 percent Jewish. The hostility between the two communities had become worse during the war because of support for the Nazis by Palestinian leaders, such as the Grand Mufti of Jerusalem. It got even worse after the war because of new waves of post-Holocaust Jewish immigrants, both legal and illegal. The Arabs wanted the door closed, the Jews wanted it open, and the British attempt

This map shows how Arab areas in Palestine were absorbed into Israel in the 1947–1949 war.

Two members of the Haganah, the Jewish militia in Palestine, in action during the fighting of 1947–1949.

to keep it slightly ajar angered everybody. Violent incidents between the two communities multiplied. Unable to find or impose a solution, the British government handed the problem over to the new United Nations in 1947.

The Birth of Israel

In November 1947, the United Nations voted to divide Palestine in two. The UN plan, however, gave Israel more than 50 percent of the territory. Rather than accept the UN partition plan, the Palestinian Arabs decided to fight. In the middle of the conflict, in May 1948, the state of Israel proclaimed its existence.

Despite immediate attacks on Israel by neighboring Arab states, the Palestinian Arabs lost the war in 1949. Egypt

The *Exodus 1947*

The British refusal to allow unlimited Jewish immigration into Palestine led to widespread smuggling of people, mostly by sea, into the region. Some boats managed to set their passengers safely ashore in Palestine, but others were intercepted by the British navy and forced to turn back. One such interception caused a worldwide sensation. Early in 1947, an old U.S. ship, the *President Warfield*, left Séte, in southern France, for Palestine, carrying about 4,500 Holocaust survivors. On leaving, the ship's name

The *Exodus* in Haifa Harbour, shortly before the ship and its Jewish refugee passengers were sent back to Europe by the British authorities in Palestine.

was changed to *Exodus 1947* in memory of the Biblical book that described the Jews' ancient flight from Egypt to Palestine.

When the ship approached the Palestinian coast, the British first tried to board it and then fired on people who resisted them, killing three and wounding many more. The ship was sent back to Europe, where its passengers wound up in the British-occupied zone of Germany. This was terrible for the survivors, but it caused a huge boost in public awareness of the Zionist cause. The story of the *Exodus 1947* produced enormous sympathy for the cause, particularly in the United States. A fictionalized account became a best-selling novel, and it was later turned into a popular Hollywood movie.

managed to seize a small area in the southwest (since known as the Gaza Strip), and Transjordan (now known as Jordan) took control of a large region bordering the Jordan River in the center (an area now called the West Bank). Israel, however, not only beat off the attacking armies but gained new territory. The conflict of 1947–1949 enlarged the territory under Israeli control by one-fourth.

A Decade of Silence

For many Jewish survivors of the Holocaust, meanwhile, the birth of Israel was the culmination of their resistance to the Nazis. Those already in the new nation were now safe behind their own borders, protected by their own army and air force. One of Israel's founding principles was that any Jew from any place could live there. Anti-Semitism might erupt anywhere in the world, but from this point on, all Jews knew that a place of safety was waiting for them. They would never again have nowhere to go.

Given this sense that Israel was a **sanctuary** from any future Holocaust, and given the fact that more than one million Jews did arrive there from post-Holocaust Europe in the late 1940s and early 1950s, it might seem inevitable that the Holocaust itself would loom large in the consciousness of the new state. This, however, was not the case. The Holocaust was not forgotten, and survivors often got together privately to discuss it, but most Israelis seemed determined to put the Holocaust behind them. They took Hebrew rather than **Yiddish** as the national language. The latter was too closely associated with their lives in central and eastern Europe and with the Holocaust that had almost ended those lives. They mastered new skills and let old European habits die out. They concentrated on creating a prosperous future and refused to dwell on the tragedies of their recent past.

It was only the trial of former Nazi Adolf Eichmann in 1961 that broke this virtual silence, brought the past rushing back, and allowed many of the survivors to come to terms with all they had been through.

CHAPTER THREE

In Pursuit of Justice

Many of the Allied troops who liberated the camps were so disgusted by what they found that they let the prisoners take their own revenge on the Nazi guards. Some prisoners did take the opportunity to humiliate or kill their persecutors, but most did not. The prisoners believed that taking violent revenge would make them little better than the Nazis. They wanted something better than that. They wanted justice.

The survivors of the Holocaust were not alone in wanting this. Millions of people had died on the battlefields of Hitler's unprovoked war, and millions more had died as a result of war crimes, such as the killing of civilians and prisoners of war. As newsreel films of the camps and their **emaciated** survivors spread around the world, people realized the depths to which the Nazis had sunk. There arose an almost universal longing to punish the people responsible for all these crimes.

First, of course, those responsible had to be identified and caught. This was far from easy. Postwar Europe was full of people who had lost any proof of their identities, and many Nazis simply abandoned their uniforms, joined the crowd, and hoped that no one would recognize them. Other Nazis escaped from Europe, usually to distant South America. Their helpers included the Swiss, Vatican, and Argentine governments. A number of Nazis also escaped justice by volunteering their services to the U.S. intelligence agencies, which then protected them.

Swift Justice

Many Nazis were caught and brought to trial in various countries. As early as November 1944, while World War II was still going on, Polish authorities tried and executed **SS** guards who had worked at Majdanek **death camp** before it was liberated. Two years later, they hanged Amon Goeth, the Plaszow labor

The Avengers

During the war, poet Abba Kovner led a resistance group inside the Vilna Ghetto in Lithuania and then a **partisan** group in the nearby Rudninkai Forest. Once the war was over, he led a group called "the Avengers," which dedicated itself to tracking down and punishing Nazi war criminals. Their aim was to poison as many as

they could. Their most notorious action occurred when they gained access to a bakery that supplied Stalag 13, a U.S.-run prison camp for Nazis in Germany, and poisoned several thousand loaves of bread. Many Nazi inmates got sick. (The group claimed hundreds died, but authorities denied it.) In 1946, Kovner and the other Avengers traveled to Palestine to take part in underground activities. After taking part in the fighting of 1947–1949, Kovner remained in Israel.

camp commandant who had used his Jewish prisoners for rifle practice. In France and Czechoslovakia, prominent people who had **collaborated** with the Nazis were tried and executed. In Germany, the United States tried and sentenced SS General Jürgen Stroop to death for shooting captured U.S. airmen. Then the US authorities handed him over to the Poles, who executed him for his role in supressing the Warsaw Ghetto uprising and in the ghetto's destruction in 1943. The British tried and executed the owner of the company responsible for producing Zyklon B, the poisonous gas used at Auschwitz.

Adolf Hitler, Joseph Goebbels, and Heinrich Himmler had all killed themselves rather than face justice. There was no such escape, however, for some other leading Nazis. Hermann Göring and twenty-one other top Nazi officials were brought to trial by the occupying powers in the German city of Nuremberg in late 1945. They were charged with starting the war ("crimes against peace"), breaking the generally accepted rules of war ("war crimes"), and the wholesale persecution and murder of civilians ("crimes against humanity"). Twelve were sentenced to death, including Göring, who managed to commit suicide before the date of his execution, which had been set for October 1946.

Victors' Laws

At the time, most people were satisfied by what became known as the Nuremberg Trials. The accused had received their day in court, the evidence had been heard, and the sentences had been handed down and carried out. It seemed that justice had been done. Even at the time, however, there were doubts about whether this was truly the case, and over the years those doubts have grown. There were three ways in which justice may not have been served by Nuremberg trials.

The first way, which most worried lawyers, was the unprecedented use of retrospective laws (laws used to prosecute actions that were not crimes at the time they were committed). Those who were on trial at Nuremberg were being tried for breaking laws that had not existed at the time they were breaking them. In addition—and this worried few people at the time but undermined the fairness of the proceedings—there was the one-sided application of these retrospective laws. They were applied only to the defeated. Soviet, U.S., and British individuals had also ordered or taken part in actions that could be considered war crimes, but none was brought to trial, let alone punished. The world was left with the impression that only losers needed to

High-ranking Nazis fill the dock at the international military tribunals in Nuremberg. Hermann Göring is seated at the near end of the front row (to the left of the white helmet). Rudolf Höss is next to him.

worry about their behavior in war. Understandably enough, few survivors of the Holocaust complained about retrospective laws or the fact that only Nazis were being punished for their war crimes. The survivors were, however, deeply concerned by the second and third ways in which justice was not served, either at Nuremberg or elsewhere.

Getting Away with Murder

The second way in which justice may not have been served concerned the general feeling that far too few of the guilty were being caught and punished. Executing a few Nazi leaders was all very well, but what about the people who had drawn up the lists, arrested the victims, driven the trains, constructed and run the camps, and turned on the gas? What about the industrialists who had made their profits from working people to death, or the army generals who had cleared the way for the murderous *Einsatzgruppen*? Why were these people not on trial?

Simon Wiesenthal (1908–)

Simon Wiesenthal was born near Lvov in what is now Ukraine. During World War II, he survived years in labor and concentration camps, but eighty-nine members of his and his wife's families died in the Holocaust. After the war, Wiesenthal began gathering evidence against the Nazis and was soon helping the U.S. authorities prosecute war criminals. During the **Cold War**, western powers lost interest in pursuing the Nazis, but Wiesenthal persisted, setting up an office from which he coordinated a worldwide hunt for known fugitives. He found Adolf Eichmann in Argentina and passed the information on to the Israeli authorities. In the 1960s, he tracked down, among others, sixteen **SS** men responsible for atrocities in Lvov, the man who arrested Anne Frank in Amsterdam, and Franz Stangl, who had been in charge of both the Treblinka and Sobibor death camps. Over the years, Wiesenthal and his organization, the Jewish Documentation Center in Vienna, Austria, have been responsible for the capture of more than one thousand Nazis. In recent years, the center has also focused on monitoring and exposing **Holocaust deniers** and present-day supporters of Nazi ideas. In 1977, the Simon Wiesenthal Center opened in Los Angeles, California. The center, honoring Wiesenthal and his work, is dedicated to preserving the memory of the Holocaust and promoting worldwide tolerance.

One explanation was that the occupying authorities were eager to put the war behind them and to concentrate on reconstruction. For this, they needed many of the people— administrators, industrialists, police—whom they might otherwise have put on trial. In addition, the occupying authorities were, by 1947, at odds with each other. The Cold War between the communist East and the **capitalist** West had begun. Both sides wanted Germans with experience in intelligence work to work for them, and the only ones available were those who

Wernher von Braun (fourth from right), led rocket research programs for Hitler's Germany and the post-war United States. He was never put on trial for his work for the Nazis during World War II.

Wernher von Braun (1912–1977)

Wernher von Braun was born in Wirsitz, a small town in Germany. After he attended the Berlin Institute of Technology in the early 1930s, his pioneering research into rocket science led to his appointment as technical director of the military testing facility at Peenemünde, where the V-2 rocket was developed in the latter stages of the war. The underground production plant in the Harz Mountains—and the rockets themselves—were built by slave laborers from a nearby concentration camp, about twenty thousand of whom were worked to death. Von Braun knew about this but did not protest. At the end of the war, he made sure that he and his principal colleagues surrendered to the Americans (rather than to the British or Soviets), because they alone had the money to fund new rocket research. Over the next quarter-century, von Braun was a central figure in developing U.S. missile and space programs. He was never charged with war crimes.

had previously worked for Hitler. Both sides wanted Germany's scientists to work for their own military programs, regardless of how those scientists had behaved in the war.

Forgotten Victims

The third and final failing of the Nuremberg process, and the one that probably affected survivors the most, was its refusal to portray the Holocaust as primarily a crime against Jews. There was a good, if misguided, reason for this—the victors did not want to adopt the Nazi attitude of seeing everything through the eyes of race. They tried to present Holocaust victims as human beings rather than as members of a particular religious or **ethnic group**. While understandable and even praiseworthy, this approach was particularly hard on the Jews, who had been persecuted more cruelly and thoroughly than the other groups.

CHAPTER FOUR

Coming to Terms with the Holocaust

Breaking through the Silence

The determination on the part of the victorious powers and the new state of Israel to look forward rather than back was both good and bad for the survivors of the Holocaust. Getting Europe moving again, sorting out the refugee problem, and beginning reconstruction helped everyone, including the Jews. By the early 1950s, the vast majority of Holocaust survivors had recovered their health, settled in new homes and countries, and started working again. The practical problems that had dominated their lives immediately after the war were largely behind them.

Other problems were much less easy to solve. Most Jewish survivors were burdened with years of terrible memories that they needed to share and understand, and the emphasis on

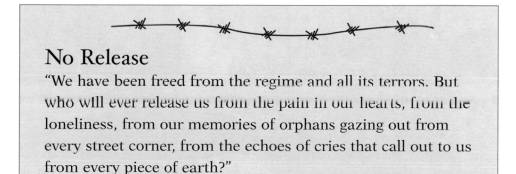

No Release

"We have been freed from the regime and all its terrors. But who will ever release us from the pain in our hearts, from the loneliness, from our memories of orphans gazing out from every street corner, from the echoes of cries that call out to us from every piece of earth?"

Dov Levin, who escaped from the Kovno Ghetto and became a partisan fighter. His parents and sisters were killed by the Nazis.

looking forward made it hard for them to do so. If they were ever to come to terms with the enormity of what had been done to them and their people, the wall of silence that surrounded the Holocaust had to be broken down.

Eichmann's Capture and Trial

The name Adolf Eichmann crops up frequently in any history of the Holocaust. It was Eichmann who supervised the emigration of Austria's Jews before World War II; Eichmann who compiled the minutes of the 1942 Wannsee Conference that coordinated the program of **genocide**; and Eichmann who tried to march the last Hungarian Jews to the **gas chambers** in the autumn of 1944. Although he never attained the highest rank in Nazi circles—he was, in essence, only an administrator—Adolf Eichmann was one of the men most responsible for the smooth operation of the Nazi murder machine.

After the war, Eichmann was twice taken into **custody**. He was never recognized, however, and on both occasions managed to escape. He worked as a chicken farmer for two years;

A witness gives testimony during the Eichmann trial in Jerusalem. Note the prisoner's uniform, held up as evidence.

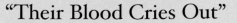

"Their Blood Cries Out"

"As I stand before you, Judges of Israel, to lead the prosecution of Adolf Eichmann, I am not standing alone. With me are six million accusers. But they cannot rise to their feet and point an accusing finger towards him who sits in the dock and cry: 'I accuse.' For their ashes are piled up on the hills of Auschwitz and the fields of Treblinka, and are strewn in the forests of Poland. Their graves are scattered throughout the length and breadth of Europe. Their blood cries out, but their voice is not heard. . . .

"Only in our generation has a nation attacked an entire defenseless and peaceful population, men and women, graybeards, children and infants, incarcerated them behind electrified fences, imprisoned them in concentration camps, and resolved to destroy them utterly."

Chief Prosecutor Gideon Hausner, speaking
at the trial of Adolf Eichmann

fled to Italy, where he lived in a monastery; and finally, with help from the Vatican, managed to escape to Argentina. He worked in a Buenos Aires car factory until Mossad, the Israeli secret service, seized him and smuggled him back to Israel in early 1960. He was brought to trial the following year, sentenced to death, and executed by hanging in May 1962.

There was enormous interest in the trial. Israelis lined up for seats in the courtroom, and schools canceled classes so that students could listen to the live radio broadcasts of the proceedings. Over several months, more than one hundred Holocaust survivors took the stand to replay their own harrowing experiences of the war years: the SS storming through the ghettos, the *Einsatzgruppen* lining up their victims, the new arrivals gathered on the ramp at Auschwitz, watching the smoke rise from the **crematorium** chimneys. Israel's years of public silence about the Holocaust were over.

Adolf Eichmann stands in court behind a protective cage. He listens as an Israeli judge confirms the death sentence pronounced five months earlier. He was hanged two days later, on May 31, 1962.

The Impact in Europe

The trial of Eichmann was also eagerly followed in Europe, where it had a similar effect. In the postwar Netherlands, for example, the Nazis were held solely responsible for the arrest and **deportation** of Dutch Jews during the war. It was argued that the Dutch people had played no part in committing these

Watching the Trial

"It was visible torture for all the witnesses to speak; one wandered in his head, screamed something wordless but terrifying to hear, fainted, remembering Auschwitz. The audience was tense, still, straining forward to listen, until now and again a voice would cry out in despair; then the police silently led the disturber from the hall. . . . The air conditioning was too cold, and yet one sweated. Every day was more than the mind and heart could bear."

Veteran war correspondent Martha Gellhorn, who reported on the Eichmann trial for Atlantic Monthly *magazine*

crimes, so what was the point of remembering or reflecting on them? After Eichmann's trial, the nation's Holocaust history became harder to ignore, and a more accurate version of events in the Netherlands began to take shape. The persecution of Dutch Jews was prominently featured in a widely watched 1960s television series called *Occupation*, and historian Jacob Presser's 1965 book *Going Under* went further, stressing how little most of his compatriots had done to help their Jewish neighbors in their hour of greatest need. In France and Italy, similar books appeared. The Holocaust had become a live issue once more, something to understand rather than something to forget.

Justice and Compensation

The search for justice and compensation continued. Every so often, in some country or other, another escaped Nazi would be unmasked, brought to trial, and sentenced. As the years went by, those on trial grew steadily older, but the eagerness for justice and retribution showed little sign of declining. The same was true of the desire for compensation or reimbursement. Much of the wealth stolen from the Jews—homes, businesses, art treasures, jewelry, even the gold from their teeth—was eventually returned or compensated for, but much was not. Some authorities, such as the postwar West German government, were quick to offer generous compensation. Others, like the Swiss banks that held Jewish assets seized during the war, fought long legal battles to block or reduce payments.

In the first British war crimes trial, former railway worker Anthony Sawoniuk—seen here leaving a British court in 1999—was convicted of murdering two Jewish women at Domachevo, Belarus, in 1942.

CHAPTER FIVE

Remembering

The new willingness to examine and discuss the Holocaust that followed the Eichmann trial was beneficial, both to the survivors (whose sufferings were at last openly acknowledged) and to the rest of humanity (which would now have a better chance of learning from the experience). Over the next thirty years, enormous efforts were made to remember, record, and explain what had actually happened during the Holocaust in all its horrifying complexity.

Where It Happened

One of the most obvious ways of fixing historical events in people's memory is the building of memorials at the places where these events occurred. The Nazis tried hard to wipe away all traces of their crimes against the Jews, but they could not destroy the sites, and many of these places now display memorials to those who perished there. The six death camps all have some kind of monument to their victims. At Belzec, for example, memorial gates shaped like strands of barbed wire lead the visitor down the old road to the site of the vanished gas chamber, where a sculpture now stands in front of an inscribed memorial. At Treblinka and Majdanek, there are small museums. At Sobibor, there is a pyramid made from the ashes of people who were killed there. Each year, about 500,000 people visit Auschwitz, where some parts of the camp complex have been preserved and other parts reconstructed.

Other much visited sites include the area in Poland where the buildings of the Warsaw Ghetto stood; the Babi Yar ravine outside Kiev in Ukraine where some 33,000 Jews were shot over several days in 1941, and the house in Amsterdam where Anne Frank and her family hid for two years. The ghetto and

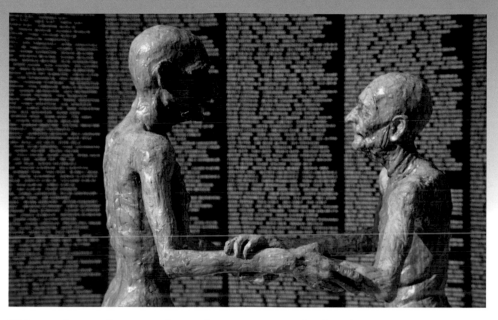

This sculpture is part of a Holocaust memorial in Miami Beach, Florida.

ravine sites illustrate how attitudes toward the Holocaust in eastern Europe and the former Soviet Union have changed in recent years. The plaques and monuments in Warsaw were almost all put up in the 1990s, while the Babi Yar memorial made no reference to the fact that the victims were Jews until after the fall of the Soviet Union in 1991.

Museums and Stamps

There are many forms of remembrance. There are now numerous museums dedicated solely to the Holocaust. The most comprehensive are probably the United States Holocaust Memorial Museum in Washington, D.C., and the Yad Vashem Holocaust Memorial complex in Jerusalem, Israel, but there are many smaller museums, exhibitions, and memorial centers throughout North America and Europe. Some museums include extensive written, audio, and film libraries.

In several European countries, January 27 (the date when Auschwitz was finally liberated) has been set aside as a day for reflecting on the lessons of the Holocaust. In the United States, Holocaust Remembrance Day is held each year on a date corresponding to the day observed in Israel as *Yom Hashoah* (*Shoah* is the Hebrew word for the Holocaust). Since the date is based on the Hebrew calendar, it varies each year, usually falling between mid-April and early May. Israel issues a new postage stamp on this date each year, and over the years many other countries have produced issues of stamps commemorating the Holocaust.

Holocaust survivor and Nobel Peace Prize winner Elie Wiesel is pictured here in 2004.

Words and Music

Since the war, and especially since the early 1960s, millions of words have been written about the Holocaust. There have been many histories and academic journals devoted to understanding what happened and why, as well as many magazine articles and books featuring first-hand accounts from the survivors. Some

A Duty to Remember

"For the survivors, remembering is a duty. They do not want to forget and, above all, they do not want the world to forget. They understand that their experiences were not meaningless, that the camps were not an accident, an unforeseeable historical happening. In every part of the world, wherever you begin by denying basic liberties, by denying equality, you move towards the camp system, and it is a road on which it is difficult to halt."

Writer Primo Levi

books—such as Primo Levi's *Survival in Auschwitz* (1961) and Elie Wiesel's *Night* (1958)—are now considered classics.

There have also been attempts to memorialize the Holocaust in poetry and music. Two famous Russians, the poet Yevgeny Yevtushenko and the composer Dmitri Shostakovich, wrote works about the massacres at Babi Yar. The U.S. composer Charles Davidson set a series of poems written by children in the camp at Theresienstadt to music, and Arnold Schoenberg wrote a musical piece about "A Survivor from Warsaw." Henryk Gorecki's Third Symphony (the *Symphony of Sorrowful Songs*), which became one of the biggest selling classical recordings of all time in the early 1990s, was written as a musical memorial to the millions murdered by the Nazis in occupied Poland.

Neighbors

In May 2000, a book called *Neighbors* was published in Poland. In it, author Jan T. Gross described how, in 1941, non-Jewish Poles in the small town of Jedwabne had massacred most of their 1,600 Jewish neighbors. The book sparked an intense debate about the country's past. Some Poles were angry—they refused to believe that such a massacre had happened and accused the Jews of inventing the story. More Poles, however, seized on the book as a way to reexamine their country's long history of anti-Semitism. In May 2001, Poland's Catholic bishops issued a public apology for wrongs committed by Catholics against Jews. Weeks later, Poles gathered in the town to hear their president, Aleksander Kwasniewski, ask the Jews' forgiveness for crimes committed by his compatriots in the years of the Holocaust. Gross's book—his act of remembrance—has stimulated the search for understanding and aided reconciliation.

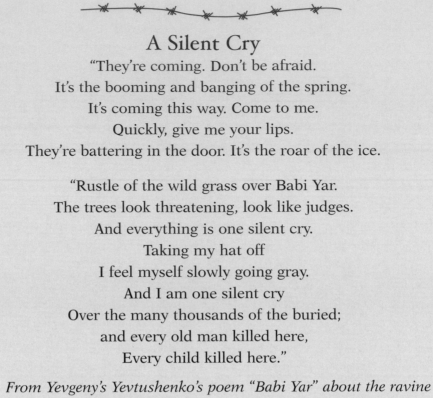

A Silent Cry

"They're coming. Don't be afraid.
It's the booming and banging of the spring.
It's coming this way. Come to me.
Quickly, give me your lips.
They're battering in the door. It's the roar of the ice.

"Rustle of the wild grass over Babi Yar.
The trees look threatening, look like judges.
And everything is one silent cry.
Taking my hat off
I feel myself slowly going gray.
And I am one silent cry
Over the many thousands of the buried;
and every old man killed here,
Every child killed here."

From Yevgeny's Yevtushenko's poem "Babi Yar" about the ravine near Kiev, Ukraine, where thousands of people—Jews and non-Jews—were murdered by Nazis

Movies and Television

Although many people have visited memorials and read works about the Holocaust, there are probably many more who learned what they know of the Holocaust from watching movies or television shows. The first major dramatization was the U.S. television miniseries *Holocaust*. As a historical account it was less than perfect, and it was criticized for over-simplification. For most viewers, however—especially those who had little knowledge of the events in question—it proved both powerful and enlightening. Some 120 million Americans watched the series in 1978, and its showing in West Germany the following year triggered a nationwide discussion that led the country to remove the statute of limitations of war crimes.

Over the last twenty-five years, only a few filmmakers have had the desire, the courage, or the commercial backing needed to tackle the subject. Claud Lanzmann's *Shoah* (1985) is maybe the most famous documentary. It tells the story of the genocide through the words of those who had experienced it, both as victims and as persecutors. Steven Spielberg's *Schindler's List* (1993), based on Thomas Keneally's book *Schindler's Ark*, was Hollywood's first big-budget movie about the Holocaust. It told the story of Oskar Schindler, the German industrialist who managed to save most of his Jewish workforce. Some critics thought that choosing a story with a German hero and a positive outcome was a strange way to represent the Holocaust, but the movie manages, in passing, to evoke the wider horror. Both *Schindler's List* and Roman Polanski's 2002 movie, *The Pianist*—which traces the fate of a young musician from the Warsaw Ghetto—won many awards and large audiences.

Oskar Schindler (played by actor Liam Neeson) addresses his Jewish workforce after securing their release from Auschwitz in the movie *Schindler's List*.

CHAPTER SIX

Questions Remaining

Not only was there a need to remember the Holocaust, there was also a need to understand it and to explain how and why something so terrible could happen. Ever since the war, both victims and historians have struggled to find satisfactory answers to certain key questions. Who, exactly, was responsible for the Holocaust? How could these people bring themselves to do something so terrible? Was there any way in which they could have been stopped? Given that it happened once, could it happen again?

Holocaust Deniers

One persistent question about the Holocaust—did it happen at all?—is essentially dishonest. Since the late 1970s, a number of so-called historians in several countries have asserted that it did not. The death camps, they claim, were just harsh labor camps; there was never any plan to exterminate the Jewish people. To support their claim, these people cite the lack of any written orders for genocide. They ignore the evidence of both survivors and persecutors, the corpses and the gas chambers, and—above all—the fact that nearly six million Jews disappeared from the face of the Earth. Their denial of the Holocaust, although without foundation, continues to be put forward in anti-Semitic literature and Web sites.

Who Was Responsible?

The question of exactly who was responsible for the Holocaust has divided historians. At one extreme, some historians claim that a few Nazis made all the key decisions and that everyone else was simply following orders, either out of habit or fear. At the other extreme are those who hold virtually the entire German people responsible and who claim that anti-Semitism

One of the gas chambers at the Majdanek death camp in eastern Poland. The blue staining was caused by the deadly gas Zyklon B.

was so deeply ingrained in the whole population that Nazi policies were carried out willingly and often enthusiastically.

The true answer must lie somewhere between these two extremes. There is plenty of historical evidence to suggest that most people do what they are told by authorities, even when their consciences suggest that they should not. On the other hand, there is some evidence that Germans who refused to take part in the Nazi-ordered atrocities were not always punished. Why, in that case, did so few stand up to the Nazis?

How Could They Have Done Something So Terrible?

Most of the people responsible for Holocaust crimes did not have to justify their actions in criminal courts. But how did they justify their actions to their families, their friends, their colleagues, and themselves? Many made the excuse that they were simply following orders out of fear or because they assumed that their government knew what it was doing. It was easier to go along than to make a fuss. Some said they were persuaded by years of anti-Semitic **propaganda** into believing

One Killer's Explanation

"I would also like to say that it did not occur to me that these orders could be unjust. It is true that I know that it is also the duty of the police to protect the innocent, but I was then of the conviction that the Jews were not innocent but guilty. I believed the propaganda that all Jews were criminals and subhumans and that they were the cause of Germany's decline after the First World War. The thought that one should disobey or evade the order to participate in the extermination of the Jews did not therefore enter my mind at all."

Kurt Mobius, who served in a police battalion unit
at Chelmno death camp

that Jews posed a real threat to the "German race." When measured against the enormity of the crime, these reasons seem completely inadequate. Put simply, we still do not know why so many Germans allowed themselves to take part in so much cruelty.

Could the Holocaust Have Been Stopped?

The Holocaust was not inevitable. When the **Great Depression** divided German society in the 1930s, the other political parties could have worked together to prevent the Nazis from seizing power. Once the Nazis had begun their persecution of the Jews, the governments of the rich western countries could have opened their borders and let the Jews in. Once the Holocaust got under way, the powerful German army could have stood up to its nation's Nazi-run government. Or the Allied forces could have taken practical action to slow or halt the Holocaust's progress by diverting some of their resources engaged in fighting World War II. At every step of the way, however, rescuing the Nazis' millions of victims somehow failed to become a priority.

Could It Happen Again?

Our inability to offer an adequate explanation of how the Holocaust happened makes it harder to guess whether it could happen again. It could be argued that it already has. In the 1970s, about 1.7 million Cambodians (21 percent of the population) were murdered by their own government. In 1994, one of Rwanda's two dominant tribes managed to wipe out one million members of the other. In 2004 and 2005, the activities of the mostly Arab Janjaweed militias against mainly dark-skinned Africans in the Darfur region of Sudan bore a striking resemblance to the activities of the Nazi *Einsatzgruppen*, the SS units that followed the German army into the Soviet Union to kill Jews and other "enemies" of the Nazis. Crimes of genocide have also been committed in post-Holocaust Europe. In the early 1990s, as Yugoslavia broke apart, Bosnian Muslims were subjected to mass killings, widespread rape, and large-scale deportations by Bosnian Serbs.

Three hundred skulls are arranged in lines outside a Rwandan chapel in November 1994. Earlier that year, about one million Tutsis had been killed by the country's other main tribal group, the Hutus.

A protester sits outside the Embassy of Sudan in Washington, D.C., August 19, 2004. She holds a sign during a rally protesting genocide in the Darfur region of Sudan.

Neo-Nazism

The Nazi beliefs and behavior that gave rise to the Holocaust are still seen today. **Racism** in general, and anti-Semitism in particular, can be found throughout the West and the Middle East. **Neo-Nazi** groups in several nations often blame problems in their societies on non-white immigrants and a worldwide conspiracy of Jews. In Germany, the Neo-Nazi movement has grown sharply in recent years. Neo-Nazi activity there ranges from attacks on immigrants—including murder—and violent street clashes to political movements. In 2004, the National Democratic Party, widely considered to be a Neo-Nazi party—earned enough votes to win government seats in the German state of Saxony. In the United States, groups such as Aryan Nations and the Ku Klux Klan provide a forum for extreme anti-Semitism and racial hatred. Neo-Nazi groups also exist in Britain, Australia, Austria, and France, among other nations.

The International Community

The idea that any government can commit atrocities within its own borders has, however, become unacceptable. Through the United Nations, people now have the ability to intervene on behalf of others who are suffering persecution and the threat of genocide. And the ability to intervene in time has been increased by improved communications. In the early 1940s, the Nazis managed to conceal the enormity of their crime for the better part of two years. A government intent on genocide in today's world would be unlikely to keep its secret for two days.

Officially Stopping Genocide

On December 9, 1948, the United Nations General Assembly passed the Convention on the Prevention and Punishment of the Crime of Genocide. Here are the first two articles of the convention:

Article 1
The Contracting Parties confirm that genocide, whether committed in time of peace or in time of war, is a crime under international law which they undertake to prevent and to punish.

Article 2
In the present Convention, genocide means any of the following acts committed with intent to destroy, in whole or in part, a national, ethnic, racial or religious group, such as: (a) killing members of the group; (b) causing serious bodily or mental harm to members of the group; (c) deliberately inflicting on the group conditions of life calculated to bring about its physical destruction in whole or part; (d) imposing measures intended to prevent births within the group.

CHAPTER SEVEN

The Legacy of the Holocaust

The consequences of the Holocaust have been far-reaching for the Jewish people. Most obviously, the Nazi genocide reduced the worldwide Jewish population by one-third, from about seventeen million in 1939 to about eleven million in 1945. It also resulted in a huge geographical shift in the world's Jewish population: While 60 percent lived in Europe in 1939, fewer

The Need to Choose

"In this haunted world of Kosovo refugees, adults wept. . . . As for their tormentors, you try to understand: how could human beings cause such agony to other human beings? Is this the lesson of our outgoing century: that it is human to be inhuman?

"Summary executions, collective punishment, forced expulsion of tens of thousands of families, frightened children separated from their parents, endless lines of desperate refugees. . . . Kosovo has entered the long and bloody list of tragedies that bring dishonor to the outgoing twentieth century.

"Surely, when human lives are involved, indifference is not an answer. Not to choose is also a choice, said the French philosopher Albert Camus. Neutrality helps the aggressor, not his victims."

*Holocaust survivor and writer Elie Wiesel in 1999, after visiting Kosovo, part of Serbia, where a portion of the population was subjected to genocidal "**ethnic cleansing**"*

Long stretches of the Israeli-built separation barrier, above, run through territory still claimed by Palestinians.

than 20 percent lived there at the end of the twentieth century. The old Jewish heartland in Poland, Byelorussia, and western Ukraine is gone; the new Jewish heartlands are Israel and the United States.

Israel and the World's Jews Today

Israel was the principal Jewish **legacy** of the Holocaust. There is, of course, no way of knowing whether a Jewish state would have come into being if the Holocaust had not taken place. There seems little doubt, however, that the Holocaust added weight to Jewish demands for such a homeland and increased the world's willingness to accept those demands.

How did the Holocaust, after it was over, affect Jews in Israel and elsewhere? It certainly left them feeling insecure, angry, betrayed, and highly sensitive to any potential threat. It also encouraged the development of Israeli characteristics, such as a fierce independence and great military ability, that would make another Holocaust impossible.

After years of conflict in the Israel-Palestine region, many Israelis hope for a more peaceful resolution with the Palestinians. They argue that if anyone should understand the plight of their dispossessed neighbors, it should be the Jews.

A Terrible Knowledge

The Holocaust has also left an impact on the rest of the world. In Germany, it left a legacy of guilt from which the country is only now emerging. Elsewhere, it gave racism the bad name it deserved. The civil rights movement in the United States and the global fight against **apartheid** in South Africa were both partly inspired by Hitler's demonstration of just how evil and

Holocaust survivors Felix Zandman (left) and Nata Osmo Gattegno (right) take part in the torch lighting during the opening ceremony of the annual Holocaust Martyrs' and Heroes' Remembrance Day at the Yad Vashem Holocaust Memorial in Jerusalem in May 2000. The Israeli flag has the six-pointed star known as the Magen David (shield, or star, of David) at its center. The torches below the flag represent the six million Jews who died during the Holocaust.

In March 2005, dignitaries gathered under the soaring roof of the Hall of Names in the recently opened Holocaust History Museum. The museum is part of the Yad Vashem Holocaust Memorial complex in Jerusalem. The Hall of Names contains the photographs and names of three million Jews.

dangerous racism could be. The acceptance in several countries of new national laws against the incitement of race hatred, and the adoption of new international laws defining and banning genocide, were also, in whole or part, legacies of the Holocaust.

The Holocaust left humankind with a terrible knowledge—or perhaps merely a reminder—of what people were capable of doing to each other. It was a denial of civilization, a clear statement that humanity had come less far than we thought it had. It was an admission that we, as humans, are less than we would like to be.

Time Line

1915 British promise to support Arab independence.
1916 Sykes-Picot Agreement.
1917 Balfour Declaration.
1920 British mandate in Palestine begins.
1933 Nazis come to power in Germany.
1942 Gassing of several million Jews in death camps begins.
1944 November: Polish authorities try and execute SS guards at Majdanek.
1945 April 30: Adolf Hitler commits suicide in Berlin.
May: World War II ends in Europe.
August: First of "the Boys" arrive in Britain.
October: Nuremberg Trials begin.
1946 Polish authorities hang Amon Goeth, commandant of Plaszow.
July 4: Forty-two Holocaust survivors are murdered in Kielce, Poland.
October: Nazi war criminals are executed after Nuremberg Trials.
1947 UN takes over responsibility for Palestine.
Exodus 1947 sails to Palestine and is turned back by the British.
Cold War begins.
November: UN votes to partition Palestine.
1947–1949 Arab-Israeli war in Palestine.
1948 May: State of Israel is founded.

1958 Elie Wiesel's *Night* is published.
1960 Adolf Eichmann is captured in Argentina and smuggled to Israel.
1961 Eichmann trial begins in Jerusalem.
Primo Levi's *Survival in Auschwitz* is published.
Yevgeny Yevtushenko's poem "Babi Yar" is published.
1962 May: Eichmann is executed.
1965 Jacob Presser's *Going Under* is published in the Netherlands.
1967 Simon Wiesenthal finds Fritz Stangl in Brazil.
1975–1979 Genocide in Cambodia.
1977 Simon Wiesenthal Center opens in Los Angeles, California.
1978 Television miniseries *Holocaust* is shown in the United States.
1985 Claud Lanzmann's documentary film *Shoah* appears.
1992–1995 Genocide in former Yugoslavia.
1993 Steven Spielberg's film *Schindler's List* is released.
United States Holocaust Memorial Museum opens in Washington, D.C.
1994 Genocide in Rwanda.
1999 Genocide in Kosovo, Serbia.
2000 Jan T. Gross's book *Neighbors* sparks national debate in Poland.
2002 Roman Polanski's film *The Pianist* is released.
2004–2005 Genocide in Sudan.

Glossary

allies: people, groups, or nations that agree to support and defend each other. "The Allies" were the nations that fought together against Germany in World War I and World War II.

anti-Semitic: expressing prejudice against Jews.

apartheid: policy in South Africa to keep non-white population separate.

capitalist: person who makes money from his or her existing capital (such as land, machinery, or money) or who favors the economic system of capitalism, under which there is private or corporate ownership of goods.

civilian: person who is not serving in the armed forces.

Cold War: period of hostility between the United States and its allies and the Soviet Union and its allies, lasting from about 1947 to 1991.

collaborate: actively assist foreign occupiers of a country.

communist: person who believes in the principles of communism, a political system in which the government owns and runs the nation's economy. (A Communist with a capital "C" is a member of the Communist Party.)

concentration camp: prison camp set up by the Nazis to hold Jews and other victims of the Nazi regime.

Many prisoners held in these camps were never tried or given a date of release.

crematorium: building in which bodies are burned.

custody: holding a person under arrest.

death camp: another term for extermination camp.

deportation: forcible removal.

Displaced Persons camp (DP camp): camp providing food and shelter for people left homeless or far from home after years of war.

***Einsatzgruppen*:** special SS units operating behind the advancing German army and ordered to murder Jews and other enemies of the Nazis.

emaciated: very thin from starvation.

emigration: leaving a country of residence to go and live somewhere else.

ethnic cleansing: murdering an unwanted ethnic group in a society.

ethnic group: group of people sharing the same national or tribal origins, language, culture, or race.

extermination camp: place set up by Nazis in which they murdered large numbers of people.

gas chamber: airtight room or other space in which people are gassed to death.

genocide: deliberate murder or attempted murder of a whole people.

Great Depression: period of worldwide economic hardship that began in late 1929 and lasted through most of the 1930s.

Gypsy: member of a group that includes the Roma and Sinti peoples, who live mostly in Europe. Gypsies are traditionally nomadic, meaning they move from place to place.

Holocaust denier: person who claims the Holocaust never happened.

homosexual: person attracted to others of the same sex.

immigrant: person who comes to a new country or region to take up residence.

immigration: entering a new country to take up residence.

labor camp: camp in which prisoners are forced to perform hard labor.

legacy: something handed down from the past.

mandate: assigned responsibility.

Middle Ages: period of European history from about A.D. 500 to 1500.

Neo-Nazi: member of a group that supports the policies and beliefs of Hitler's Nazi Party.

partisan: fighter who lives and fights behind enemy lines or within occupied territory.

propaganda: promotion and spreading of ideas, often involving either a selective version of the truth or plain lies.

racism: prejudice against people because of their race.

refugee: person who flees or is forced to leave his or her own home or country and who seeks refuge elsewhere.

sanctuary: place of refuge.

SS: short for *Schutzstaffel*, a Nazi elite force also known as "the blackshirts."

terrorist: person who performs acts of violence in order to make a political point or force a change in government policy.

traumatize: to deeply shock and upset.

Yiddish: language of the Jews in eastern Europe that includes elements of Hebrew, German, and Slavic languages.

Zionism: movement to reestablish a Jewish state in the Holy Land.

Further Resources

Books

Altman, Linda Jacobs. *Crimes and Criminals of the Holocaust* (The Holocaust in History). Enslow Publishers, 2004.

Altman, Linda Jacobs. *Impact of the Holocaust* (The Holocaust in History). Enslow Publishers, 2004.

Brager, Bruce L. *The Trial of Adolf Eichmann: The Holocaust on Trial* (Famous Trials). Lucent Books, 1999.

Sheehan, Sean. *After the Holocaust* (The Holocaust). Hodder & Stoughton, 2001.

Shuter, Jane. *Aftermath of the Holocaust* (The Holocaust). Heinemann Library, 2003.

Web Sites

The Holocaust: Crimes, Heroes and Villains
www.auschwitz.dk
Web site about those involved in the Holocaust, with biographies, poetry, photos, and more.

The Holocaust History Project
www.holocaust-history.org
Archive of documents, photos, and essays on various aspects of the Holocaust.

Holocaust Survivors
www.holocaustsurvivors.org
Interviews, photos, and sound recordings of survivors of the Holocaust.

The Museum of Tolerance's Multimedia Learning Site
motlc.wiesenthal.org
Educational Web site of the Simon Wiesenthal Center, a Jewish human rights agency.

Non-Jewish Holocaust Victims
www.holocaustforgotten.com
A site dedicated to the Nazis' five million non-Jewish victims.

United States Holocaust Memorial Museum
www.ushmm.org
Personal histories, photo archives, and museum exhibits of the Holocaust.

About the Author

David Downing has been writing books for adults and children about political, military, and cultural history for thirty years. He lives in Britain.

Index